A Great Idea

Recycled Tires

by Toney Allman

NORWOOD HOUSE PRESS

Norwood House Press
PO Box 316598
Chicago, Illinois 60631

For information regarding Norwood House Press, please visit our Web site at:

www.norwoodhousepress.com or call 866-565-2900.

LIBRARY OF CONGRESS CATALOGING-IN-PUBLICATION DATA

Allman, Toney.
   Recycled tires / by Toney Allman.
      p. cm. — (A great idea)
   Includes bibliographical references and index.
   Summary: "Describes the invention and development of recycled rubber tires.
Includes glossary, Web sites, and bibliography for further reading"—Provided by
publisher.
   ISBN-13: 978-1-59953-197-7 (library edition : alk. paper)
   ISBN-10: 1-59953-197-6 (library edition : alk. paper)
1. Waste tires—Management—Juvenile. 2. Recycling—Juvenile. I. Title.
TD797.7.A55 2008
678'.320286—dc22
                                                                    2008015736

Manufactured in the United States of America.

Contents

Note: Words that are **bolded** in the text are defined in the glossary on page 42.

Chapter 1

Too Many Old Tires

On October 31, 1983, a terrible fire started in a tire dump in Winchester, Virginia. Seven million old tires piled 80 feet (24m) high burned on 5 acres (2ha). Black smoke rose thousands of feet into the air. People in four states could see the smoke. The smoke carried dangerous chemicals from the burning tires. Ash fell on people and towns up to 5 miles (8km) away. On the ground, the oil and tar in the tires melted. It ran into the earth and a creek nearby. The oil and tar poisoned the soil and water.

The Dangers of Tire Fires

The danger to people and the **environment** was high. So the U.S. government stepped in to help. The **Environmental Protection Agency** (EPA) sent an emergency team to help fight the fire. The firefighters had

Old tires burn out of control at an outdoor storage lot. Poisonous substances from the burned tires leak into the earth and cause pollution in the air.

the fire under control within a few days. But they could not put it out completely. The tires burned and **smoldered** for more than eight months. Finally on July 14, 1984, the fire was declared out. But the problems did not end there. It took years to clean up the poisons in the creek and earth.

This was not the first or only fire in a tire dump. In Ontario, Canada, in 1990, a fire burned 17 million tires. It was the largest tire fire in history. People 260 miles (418km) away in Cleveland, Ohio could

Billowing black smoke covers the sky during a tire fire.

see the smoke plume. Hundreds of firefighters battled the blaze. It took them 17 days to put out the fire. In that time, 264,000 gallons (999,050L) of oil from the melted tires ran over the ground. It took many weeks to clean up all the burned oil.

In 1998 one of the largest tire fires in the United States started in Tracy, California. Seven million tires were piled in a huge 20-acre (8ha) pit. A nearby grass fire spread to the mound of tires. Flames and smoke rose 70 feet (21m) into the air. Firefighters got the largest flames under control. They were able to prevent the fire from spreading. But even after months of work, they could not put out the fire completely. They decided to let the tires smolder. They did not want water from their hoses to wash poisons from the tires into nearby streams,

Did You Know?

Experts estimate that 270 million vehicle tires are thrown away each year in the United States.

creeks, and **groundwater**. For two years the tires smoked and smoldered. People could smell the tires from miles away, and they stank! Finally, the fire burned itself out. But California had to spend $365,000 to clean up the polluted pit.

Tires, Tires Everywhere

Old tire dumps used to be dangerous places. Thousands of them existed all

over America. People just threw tires away and let them pile up anywhere. In 1990 the EPA reported that between two billion and three billion old tires were lying around in the United States.

Fires were not the only problem resulting from all of these old tires. Rainwater collected inside them, and mosquitoes bred in that water. Rats and snakes made homes in tire dumps. The tires were ugly to look at, and they polluted the environment. Even city **landfills** did not want the used tires. Some city landfills took them, but some refused to accept them. They took up too much space. They trapped gases that escaped from rotting garbage at the landfill. The gases made the tires so light that sometimes they rose to the surface even when they were buried. No one seemed to know what to do with all of these old tires. The best answer seemed to be **recycling**. But that was not as easy as it sounded.

Emergency responders attend to a fire caused by burning tires. Tire fires can spread rapidly.

Too Tough to Reuse

When cars and tires were first invented, tires were made of natural rubber. It came from the sap of rubber trees. To make tires, the rubber was vulcanized. This meant it was heated and mixed with a chemical called sulfur. The process made the tires **weatherproof** and tough. But the tires could not be melted down to form new tires. When heated, the sulfur-treated rubber became weak. It was too weak for making new tires.

Who Thought of That?

Charles Goodyear invented vulcanization in 1839. Before that time, rubber had few uses. It made good pencil erasers but not good shoes, raincoats, or patching materials. It became solid and cracked in cold weather. It melted into a gooey mess in hot weather. Goodyear thought he could change that. He tried mixing rubber with many different chemicals. He wanted to see if it could be made stable no matter what the weather. For years, he failed.

Then one day, he went to a store to show his friends something he had made. It was a ball of rubber and sulfur. His friends laughed at him. This angered Goodyear. As he yelled and waved his arms around, the rubber ball flew out of his hands. It landed on a potbellied stove. Goodyear tried to scrape it off and made a great discovery. The heat had changed his wad of rubber and sulfur. It did not melt. It was charred and hard. Goodyear had found the way to weatherproof rubber—heat plus sulfur. Goodyear died in 1860. This was long before car tires were made. But the Goodyear Tire Company was named in his honor.

There was only one way to recycle the tires. They could be ground up and mixed with pure tree rubber. The mix of sulfur-rubber and pure, strong rubber could be used for making more tires.

But by the 1960s even this was no longer possible. Natural rubber was not being used for making tires anymore. Scientists had learned how to make synthetic rubber. Synthetic rubber is made from chemicals that act like natural rubber. It is cheap and easy to use for tires. Other improvements followed. Tire companies invented steel **radial tires**. The steel threads in the radial tires made the tires even tougher and safer for cars.

All of these changes were good for drivers. But they were not good for the environment. The new tires could not be recycled. The steel threads and other **ingredients** used in making tires were the

Dr. Wallace H. Carothers, shown here, was a chemist who led the development of synthetic rubber in the 1930s.

Did You Know?

When scrap tires collect water, they form an ideal breeding ground for mosquitoes. During breeding season, this can amount to anywhere from 10,000 to 1 million mosquitoes per tire.

problem. There was no good way to separate all of the ingredients from the rubber so it could be used again. So most old tires were just thrown away. By 1990, when the tire dump in Ontario burned, only 17 percent of old tires were recycled.

Trying for an Answer

Still, recycling tires seemed like a good way to get rid of tire dumps. The EPA wanted to recycle more tires. So did the United States **Congress**. In 1991 Congress passed a law that said the states must use a mix of ground rubber and **asphalt** to repave and repair state highways. Congress hoped this would reduce at least some of the problems with **scrap** tires.

It was a good idea, but it did not work. Patches made from the mixture of ground rubber and asphalt did not last. In Georgia, for instance, the mixture was used on part of a highway near Atlanta. After four years,

Perfect for the Feet

In the villages of Mexico and the jungles of Southeast Asia, people have been recycling tires for decades. They make sandals out of them. Rubber-soled huaraches helped Mexican Indians beat runners in foot races in the United States. Sandals for Vietnamese soldiers had soles cut from tires with straps made from inner tubes. The sandals are so tough that they can last for twenty years. They dry quickly when wet and protect feet from sharp stones and burrs.

A Very Bad Idea

In the 1970s Florida and the U.S. government came up with a way to recycle tires. They decided to build a huge reef off the coast of Florida. It was made out of 2 million tires. The tires were tied together with steel, nylon clips, and bands. It was named the Osborne Reef. People thought the reef would be good for the environment. They thought it would give fish and other sea life a good home.

They were wrong. The tire reef turned out to be a terrible mistake. The steel rusted and broke in the seawater. The tires floated apart. The small sea creatures using them for a home all died. Then storms tossed the tires around in the water. The tires banged into nearby coral reefs, damaging and killing them. Other tires sank and lay in the sand on the ocean floor. They were spread out over 34 acres (13.8ha) of the seabed. Today, Florida and the U.S. Coast Guard are still working to clean up and remove those tires.

the rubber mixture turned **brittle** and cracked. The cost was also a problem. The new mixture cost twice as much as regular asphalt cement for patching highways. Many states refused to use the ground rubber. It just had too much junk in it to be useful, and it cost too much. Congress **repealed** the law in 1993. But an idea had been born. More and more people started thinking about how to recycle old tires.

Chapter 2

An Idea Gets Rolling

Charles McDonald came up with an idea for patching holes in the road in the 1960s. At the time, he was an inspector for the Arizona highway department. He traveled to sites where construction crews were working on roads. He checked the work to make sure it was done properly. His job required a lot of travel. Often, McDonald was too far from home to drive back at night. But he did not want

So Much to Recycle

There are about 671 million vehicles in the world. If each vehicle uses up three sets of tires in its lifetime, the world will have more than 8 billion tires to recycle. Each car tire contains about 2.5 gallons (9.5L) of oil and 2.5 pounds (1kg) of steel. That is a lot of rubber, oil, and steel to throw away. But the Rubber Manufacturers Association says that recycling is stopping the waste. Today, 110 different products are being made with recycled tires.

Hundreds of miles of highway stretch throughout Arizona. The dry climate cracks the asphalt, requiring the roads to be patched.

to stay in hotels. So he hooked a small travel trailer to the back of his car. That way, he could camp out at a road construction site until his inspections were done. And then he could head straight to the next site.

The only problem with this plan was a leaky roof. Whenever it rained, the roof of his trailer leaked. This posed a bit of a problem for McDonald. At some point, he noticed all of the old, used tires from the road equipment. They had just been tossed aside, out of the way. Seeing those old tires gave McDonald an idea for patching his leaky roof. He thought he might be able to use some of those old tires to make a patch.

The Search for a Patch

McDonald experimented with things he found at the construction sites. He tried mixing asphalt, oil, and shredded tires. The tire rubber was stretchy and flexible. After a few tries, he came up with a sticky roofing mixture. When it was heated, it could be spread on the trailer roof. It worked well. Once he had patched the holes, the roof stopped leaking.

McDonald could have stopped there. But he kept thinking about his roof patch. He wondered if the same mixture could be used to patch holes in the roads. The mixture would work like a stretchy bandage to seal the patches. Back at home, he began experimenting with his mixture again. Finally, he invented a patching mixture that stuck to road pavement.

Potholes require constant patching. They are common hazards on asphalt roads.

The Arizona highway department used McDonald's patching mixture for many years. But it was not practical in many other places. Most of Arizona is warm in the winter and very hot in the summer. Some parts do get very cold in winter but not like in the northern states or Canada. In those places, McDonald's patching mixture did not work. It cracked and separated. And the chemicals in the shredded tires added to the problem. The tires could not be shredded finely enough to mix well with the asphalt. So, McDonald's invention did not get much notice outside of Arizona.

Machines Equal to the Task

That changed in the 1990s. People began to look at McDonald's ideas in a new way. Some developed new machines. These machines could grind

A Department of Transportation worker in Arizona fills potholes with a patching mixture made of asphalt and rubber.

tires into tiny pieces. The pieces were much smaller than anything done in the past. The Wendt Corporation in New York sold the first complete set of tire recycling machines in the United States in 2002. The set includes a Super Chopper that can chop even large truck tires into 6-inch (15cm) pieces. Then these pieces are fed into a Heavy Rasper. This machine shreds the rubber into 3/4-inch (1.9cm) pieces. It also uses a device that pulls out almost all of the steel wire. Two machines called granulators cut the pieces into smaller and smaller grains of rubber. When the last granulator is finished, the tire shreds are less than 1/8-inch (0.3cm) large. These finished tiny grains are called crumb rubber.

Another company has come up with an even better way of making crumb rubber. Recovery Technologies Corporation of Canada shreds the tires and then freezes them. The frozen chunks become brittle and as easy to shatter as ice. And that's exactly what happens next. The frozen shredded tires are sent to an area called the "hammer mill." There, they are smashed to bits. Then one machine sucks

A conveyor belt is used to carry recycled tires into special machines that will chop and shred them.

Making Asphalt Rubber

Modern asphalt rubber can be made right at construction sites. The huge machines that mix and heat the asphalt and rubber are like factories on wheels. One company, CEI Enterprises, makes the Asphalt Rubber Blending System. It mixes and stirs the asphalt and ground rubber. It can mix 35 tons (32mt) of asphalt and ground rubber per hour. Then the mixture goes to a 25,000-gallon (94,600L) tank where it is heated and cured. Finally the hot asphalt rubber can be poured on the road.

Crumb rubber has gone through other changes to make it more usable. One of these came about in 1999. A scientist from Australia, Dong Yang Wu, treated crumb rubber with special chemicals. These chemicals made the rubber bind with or grab hold of materials such as asphalt. This prevented cracking.

Shredded rubber lies in a heap after the first phase of recycling. The shredded rubber will then be ground into fine crumb rubber.

out the unneeded fibers, and a large magnet removes the steel wires. The tiny rubber pieces are ground again. The resulting crumb rubber is so clean and fine that it looks like dirt or powder.

Paving U.S. Highways

Making pavement for roads was the first real use for recycled tires. McDonald's process works well with today's fine, clean, crumb rubber. The crumb rubber is heated, blended, and cooked with other materials, such as oil. Then it can be treated with chemicals and mixed with asphalt to make strong, safe roads. The ma-

Did You Know?

California and Arizona use more asphalt rubber in highway road projects than all the other states. Florida is the next largest user.

terial is called asphalt rubber. It is used today for paving whole highways. In 2007, 220 million pounds (99.8 million kg) of crumb rubber were used to pave highways in the United States. That amounts to about 12 million old tires that were recycled instead of being thrown away.

Road pavement is just one of the many uses for crumb rubber.

The world is filled with piles of old tires. Once recycled, these scrap tires will find new life as many other different products.

Paving roads with asphalt rubber costs more than regular asphalt. But asphalt rubber does not crack in the cold. It is stretchy and flexible. It is even safer for drivers. Tires stick a little to asphalt rubber, and cars do not skid as easily in the rain. Overall, roads paved with asphalt rubber last longer and need fewer repairs.

Solving a Problem

Modern crumb rubber is still used for paving roads. But experts are also finding other uses for bits of old tires. And in the process, they are helping the world solve the problem of too many old tires. In 2005, 87 percent of scrap tires were used for some other purpose. Most were burned for fuel in factories and power plants. But many millions of old tires now make helpful products for people.

Chapter 3

Crumb Rubber in All Kinds of Places

Miles of Arizona roads are now paved with bits of old tires. The state had topped and patched many roads with asphalt rubber over the years. But none of this work involved city freeways until 2002. That year, the Arizona Department of Transportation (ADOT) repaved 12 miles (19km) of freeway in Phoenix. Workers laid a 1-inch (2.5cm) topping of asphalt rubber over the concrete.

Did You Know?

About 300,000 pounds (136,077kg) of crumb rubber (sometimes mixed with sand) is applied to the typical football or soccer field before it is covered with artificial grass.

Earthships

Some people do not need crumb rubber to recycle tires. Earthships are houses built entirely of used, whole tires. The tires are stacked in a horseshoe shape and filled with dirt. The walls and ceilings of earthships may be plastered with mud or covered with cement for insulation and to make them solid. Near Taos, New Mexico, a housing development of about sixty houses has been built. Every house is an earthship. The thick tire walls keep homes cool during the hot desert days. They also hold heat inside during cold nights.

An earthship stands in the desert landscape of Taos, New Mexico. There are an estimated 1,000 earthships in existence around the world.

A Pleasant Surprise

When this project was done, ADOT got a pleasant surprise. People living beside the freeway were thrilled with the new material. They used to be bothered by the loud rumble of all those tires on the road. Now, with the asphalt rubber, the traffic sounds had faded away. Tires on asphalt rubber were much quieter than anyone ever realized.

All over Phoenix, people asked for the new quiet asphalt rubber to be laid near their homes. In 2003 ADOT began its Quiet Pavement Program. ADOT says that 75 percent of freeway noise is caused by tires on regular pavement. Experts call this noise "tire slap." Tires make this noise as they hit the road surface over and over. Asphalt rubber can reduce this noise a lot. Under the Quiet Pavement Program, ADOT paved 115 miles (185km) of freeway with asphalt rubber. It has paved more than 3,000 miles (4,828km) of other roadways throughout the state with asphalt rubber. Other states have also started quiet pavement programs. Among them are California, Nevada, New Mexico, and Washington.

Making a Difference

In Washington, the road tests began with asphalt rubber in 2006. Washington State Department of Transportation (WSDOT) paved short stretches of highway with asphalt rubber. WSDOT worried about how rain would affect the new pavement. Parts of Washington get a lot of rain. No one was sure how long the pavement would last. People who

In Seattle, Washington, people sleep better thanks to freeways that are paved with sound-muffling asphalt rubber.

live near these projects hope it lasts a long time.

In 2007 WSDOT paved 2.25 miles (3.6km) of State Highway 520. The state asked residents nearby how quiet the new pavement was, because so many people live close to this part of the highway. The residents said the asphalt rubber had made a huge difference. They said the asphalt rubber makes road noise sound twice as far away as it really is. Even people riding in cars say the road noise is less when they hit this stretch of highway.

The Detroit Lions' Ford Field, shown here, uses crumb rubber under its artificial turf for a softer playing surface.

Run, Hit, and Tackle

Crumb rubber is not just making a difference on highways. It is also showing up on playing fields around the country. When NFL teams play at Ford Field in Detroit, Michigan, they play on fake grass. And under the fake grass is fake dirt. The grass is known as "artificial turf." The dirt is crumb rubber. And the NFL's Detroit Lions are not the only team playing on a crumb rubber surface.

Crumb rubber is underfoot on more than 1,000 playing and practice fields around the country. In the NFL alone, crumb rubber fields are used by the Dallas Cowboys, the Denver Broncos, the Seattle Seahawks, and the New York Giants, among others. Some college sports teams and professional baseball teams also play on crumb rubber.

Athletes and trainers say the crumb rubber surface is easier on their bones and joints. Older surfaces were like playing on concrete, as there was no give.

Some high schools are also switching to crumb rubber playing surfaces. Pioneer High School and Huron High School are located in Ann Arbor, Michigan. Both schools now have playing fields with crumb rubber surfaces. These changes were made with help from the Ford Motor Company. This car company has been working on ways to reuse and recycle old car tires and other car parts for a long time.

Trot and Canter

Ballplayers are not the only athletes who benefit from crumb rubber surfaces. Horses and riders are also working out on crumb rubber surfaces. Many show rings and practice arenas in the United States and Canada have switched from dirt to crumb rubber. One of these is Brookwood Equestrian Center in Tacoma, Washington. "The horses are happier . . . and not as tired at the end of the day," says a spokesman for the center. This is because crumb rubber is softer than dirt. Because it is softer, the shock of the horses' hooves

A man holds clean, ultrafine crumb rubber in his hands.

less slippery than dirt. So, horses are less likely to fall. This protects riders from spills, too. And when a rider does fall or jumps off a horse quickly, the impact is softer than hitting dirt. "The pain associated with falling off is almost nothing compared to a similar fall in a conventional sand ring," says a spokesman with an indoor horse arena in Ontario, Canada.

Just Have Fun

striking the surface is less. So the horses have less pain and fewer **injuries**.

Crumb rubber is also safer for horses and riders. Even in the rain, the surface is

Falling is something kids know a lot about. And lots of kids fall on playgrounds. About 550,000 injuries occur on playgrounds every year. Most of these injuries result from falls on hard surfaces. These include gravel, dirt, wood chips, or

But Is the Playground Safe?

Some concerned citizens worry that crumb rubber is bad for the environment and for human health. They point out that crumb rubber is still vulcanized. And it still has chemicals that could leak into the soil. They also worry about fumes. They are concerned that fumes from crumb rubber playground surfaces might harm kids who breathe them. Kids sometimes come home from playgrounds with bits of crumb rubber stuck in their hair or clothes.

The EPA says that crumb rubber seems safe. It has no reports of sicknesses in kids at the playgrounds. Tests show only a little leaking of chemicals into the ground. The EPA says that crumb rubber is not poisonous or dangerous. Many people think that more studies need to be done.

pavement. How hard a person hits the ground in a fall is called "shock impact." Crumb rubber helps to reduce shock impact. Because it is soft, it cushions falls.

At Illini Bluffs Elementary School in Illinois, the playground was covered with crumb rubber in 2002. The principal said that some students had broken bones on the old playground. Since the school put in crumb rubber, not one student has been injured. Experts have shown that crumb rubber is safe for kids. In one study, scientists dropped an egg from 12 feet (4m) high onto a crumb rubber surface. The egg bounced, but it did not break.

Many kids prefer crumb rubber to sand or gravel. It is easier to run on crumb rubber than on sand or gravel. Crumb rubber

Workers give a playground a new surface of crumb rubber in Detroit, Michigan.

day life. People can buy shoes that have soles made from crumb rubber. They can find floor mats for their cars, mouse pads

Happy Feet

The Withlacoochee State Trail is a hiking and biking trail in Florida. It follows an old railway. It runs through state parks, wildlife preserves, forests, and wetlands. It is 46 miles (74km) long. It is one of the first trails in the United States to be paved entirely with crumb rubber. People who use the trail find it comfortable. It is easy on legs and feet because the rubber is bouncy and spongy. Some users say that hiking or biking on the trail is like walking or riding on air.

comes in lots of colors for playgrounds, too. One company has blue, purple, and red crumb rubber for playgrounds as well as plain black or brown.

Recycled Lifestyles

Crumb rubber is not just for outdoor surfaces. It is fast becoming a part of every-

Roof tiles made of fire-resistant crumb rubber can last for decades.

that last for fifty years. These roofs resist fire. They do not burn as easily as wood **shingles** do. Crumb rubber can be formed into bricks to make garden paths and patios, too. People are discovering that crumb rubber is a great way to recycle old tires.

for their computers, and pedals for their bikes—all made with crumb rubber. To make these items, the crumb rubber is heated. Then it is mixed with other materials. This mixture is then molded and shaped into different items.

Crumb rubber is even used in people's homes. Crumb rubber tiles make roofs

Chapter 4

Recycling Tomorrow

Australian scientist John Dobozy has a recipe for using old tires. He came up with his recipe in 2003. That is when he developed a way to cook old tires. He uses a giant microwave oven. As the tires cook, they break down into some of their original ingredients. These include oil, rubber, fabric, and steel. All of these ingredients can be reused in some way or another.

Did You Know?

Before John Dobozy settled on a microwave oven for cooking old tires, he tried barbecuing them. This idea did not work. The oil escaped from the tires, and the neighbors complained about the foul smell.

John Dobozy

John Dobozy started a company to recycle whole tires. His company is called Molectra Technologies. Dobozy believes recycling tires is an important way to protect the environment. He won the Australian "2005 Invention of the Year" for his recycling process. He won an "Eco-Tech" award for his invention in Japan in 2005. On his company's Web site, he says, "The art of recycling is to [imitate] nature's process of recreating useful compounds from the elements of the Earth."

Dobozy sets some of the oil aside. He uses it to make more rubber. He starts this process by chopping up the cooked rubber. Then he soaks it in an oil bath for a long time. He says the soaked rubber becomes as soft as cream cheese. It can be used like crumb rubber. Or it can be molded into new items such as floor tiles or tires for wheelbarrows.

Dobozy's goal is to make use of the whole scrap tire, not just the rubber. He hopes that someday his method will be used worldwide to recycle tires. Dobozy is one of many scientists who are thinking about ways of recycling old tires. Some, like Dobozy, are trying to find ways to recycle all the ingredients in old tires, not just the rubber. Others are looking into new ways of using crumb rubber.

Use It in a New Way

In 2006 scientist Yuefeng Xie at Penn State University found a way to filter (or clean) dirty water with crumb rubber.

This typical wastewater treatment system relies on sand and rocks. Scientists someday hope to use crumb rubber for cleaning wastewater.

Usually sand or bits of rock are used to clean **wastewater**. Wastewater passes through pipes that contain sand or rocks. As the water flows through the pipes, the sand or rocks trap bits of dirt. The filtered water keeps flowing but sometimes leaves clogged pipes behind.

Xie thinks crumb rubber would do a better job of filtering wastewater than sand or rocks. Crumb rubber bends and flexes. Even when it clumps, tiny air spaces remain between the bits of rubber. These would let the water pass through while still catching the dirt.

Xie has tried this in his lab. He has not yet tried it in the real world. But he thinks it would work. It could be used for filtering water on ships, in city water treatment

Nobody Has Proven It Will Work

Michael Blumenthal is a member of the Rubber Manufacturers Association. He says that devulcanizing rubber has never been proven to work on a large scale. It costs too much money. It costs more to devulcanize tires than the rubber is worth. People have been trying for years. But no one has succeeded in the real world. Many scientists say that vulcanization cannot be fully reversed.

Blumenthal still hopes for a method that will work. Only then can new tires be made out of old tires. And only then can the goal of recycling all of the world's old tires be achieved.

Devulcanization

Inventing new uses for crumb rubber is a good way to recycle. But some scientists want a better way to recycle scrap tires. Even when tires are ground up, they are still vulcanized. So the rubber is still mixed and blended with sulfur. That is why it is not as useful as brand-new rubber. Scientists want to get pure rubber.

New tires are stacked in storage. If rubber could be easily devulcanized, new tires could be made from old tires.

plants, and even in disaster areas where clean water has been polluted by storms or earthquakes.

Then they could do anything with the rubber—even make new tires. New tires from old tires would be the perfect recycling system.

Some scientists want to find a way to devulcanize rubber. This would not be easy to do. Devulcanizing rubber is like trying to unbake a cake. It is like trying to restore a cake to its original ingredients. That means getting back the flour, sugar, eggs, and butter so that each ingredient can be used again.

The problem with this idea is that the ingredients change once they become part of the cake. Eggs, for example, are changed when they are beaten and cooked. And if you mixed flour in your eggs, it would make a bad-tasting omelet. The same is true with vulcanized rubber.

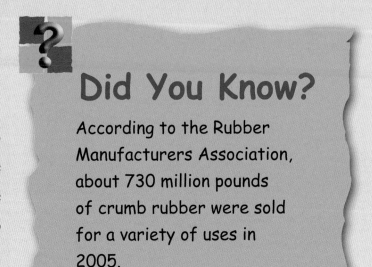

Did You Know?

According to the Rubber Manufacturers Association, about 730 million pounds of crumb rubber were sold for a variety of uses in 2005.

Rubber that has been vulcanized is forever changed, just like eggs in a cake batter. And rubber mixed with sulfur makes a bad tire, much like the omelet mixed with flour. The tire is weak and does not last on rough roads. Holes appear or treads wear away. Only devulcanizing the rubber can make it as good as new. This is not an easy job, but scientists around the world are trying.

In 1999 Larry Hunt and Ron Kovalak worked for the Goodyear tire company. They invented a way of devulcanizing tires. They used chemicals called solvents. Solvents help other substances dissolve. For instance, when sugar mixes with water, the sugar dissolves. In that case, water is a solvent.

Hunt and Kovalak used strong solvents to partly dissolve the rubber in old tires. They then heated the rubber with powerful microwaves. This gave them 40 percent of the pure rubber out of the tires.

This process works in the lab but has not been put to the test in the real world. However, the idea of devulcanizing tires has some promise.

With Heat and Sound

Green Rubber Global is one of the companies that thinks devulcanizing tires is a good idea. But it does not use solvents to do it. It has tried another method. This company uses chemicals that make crumb rubber expand. Then the rubber is heated until the sulfur separates from the rubber.

Many people are excited about its method for devulcanizing tires. One of its supporters is actor Mel Gibson. He is active in efforts to protect and save the environment. Gibson asked the town of Gallup, New Mexico, to help the plant get started. He believes it will help the environment. Some experts are not sure the process will work. They are also concerned that it will cost too much money

Actor Mel Gibson, left, and others study an airplane engine in 2007. Gibson is a financial supporter of Green Rubber Global's proposed devulcanization plant in Gallup, New Mexico.

even if it does work. No one knows yet if the plant will be a success.

Avraam I. Isayev is a scientist at the University of Akron in Ohio. He also thinks devulcanizing old tires has promise. His idea is to use powerful sound waves, or ultrasound. The ultrasound would break down the rubber. It would separate the bonds between the rubber and the sulfur. The result would be rubber that is about 70 percent as pure as new synthetic rubber. But it would not be as strong as new rubber.

Yum, Yum, Sulfur!

There are many other ideas being tested. Some scientists have found a way to use **bacteria** to devulcanize rubber. They use special kinds of bacteria that eat sulfur. These types of bacteria mostly live in hot springs, such as the ones in Yellowstone National Park. These bacteria live in the hot water of the springs. They use sulfur for their food and energy. They can be grown in the lab. Then they are given crumb rubber to eat. They eat the sulfur, leaving the rubber behind.

Using bacteria to devulcanize rubber works, but it is hard to do. And it costs a lot of money. It is hard to keep the bacteria alive. They can only live at certain temperatures. And, it can take hundreds of days for the bacteria to eat the sulfur. Once they are done, the bacteria must be filtered out of the mixture.

Bacteria that thrive in the hot springs of Yellowstone Park may one day help with devulcanization by eating the sulfur found in rubber.

A Use for Every Tire

So far, no one knows the best way to devulcanize rubber. But most scientists believe the answer will come. When it does, who knows how tires will be used? Maybe someday, you will wear clothing or live in a house made from old tires. And then tire dumps will become a thing of the past.

Glossary

asphalt: A mixture used for paving.

bacteria: Tiny organisms that can only be seen through microscopes.

brittle: Hard but easily broken.

Congress: A lawmaking body of the U.S. government. It is made up of senators and representatives elected from all fifty states.

environment: Surroundings, especially those necessary to live, such as the earth, air and water.

Environmental Protection Agency: An arm of the U.S. government with the goal of protecting human health and the environment.

groundwater: Water lying below the earth's surface.

ingredients: The parts in a mixture or combination.

injuries: Wounds.

landfills: Lowlands built up with alternating layers of trash and earth.

radial tires: Tires with layers or cords of rubber-coated steel fibers running at right angles to the belts of rubber and wrapped around them.

recycling: Converting waste into a form in which it can be reused.

repealed: A law that is made and then canceled.

scrap: Something that has been thrown away.

shingles: Rectangular pieces of wood or other material used for roofing.

smoldered: Burned slowly with smoke but no flame.

wastewater: Water that has been used for washing, flushing, or soaking and therefore contains waste products and dirt.

weatherproof: Cannot be damaged by rain, wind, cold, or heat.

For More Information

Books

Carrie Gleason, *How Did That Get Here? The Biography of Rubber*. New York: Crabtree, 2005. Readers follow the life of rubber from the discovery of natural rubber to how its discovery changed the world to how synthetic rubber came to be, and to how the use of rubber affects the environment.

Sally Hewitt, *Waste and Recycling*. New York: Crabtree, 2008. Readers can learn about how trash affects the earth and what each person can do to reduce waste and help the planet.

Helen Orme, *Garbage and Recycling*. New York: Bearport, 2008. This book discusses the problems with landfills and too much garbage. It explains how recycling can save the environment.

Charlotte Wilcox, *Cool Science: Recycling*. Minneapolis: Lerner, 2007. The author describes recycling efforts with many different products and includes a section on recycling tires.

Web Sites to Visit

GreenMan Technologies (www.greenman.biz). This recycling company has a slide show on its home page that follows scrap tires from an ugly dump to a beautiful playground.

How Landfills Work (http://people.how stuffworks.com). With plenty of pictures, this long article explains in detail how a landfill is built and operated.

Recycling Tires Can Be Fun (http://eco bites.com/diy-recycling-projects/recycling-tires-can-be-fun.html). This site has a lot of good ideas about ways people can recycle old tires. Visitors can learn to make swings, sandals, and much more from used tires.

Index

Picture Credits

Cover: © Ilene MacDonald/Alamy; AP Photo/Albuquerque Journal, Adolphe Pierre-Louis, 40; AP Photo/Amy E. Powers, 27; AP Photo/Dan Loh, 29; AP Photo/Eric Draper, 25; AP Photo/Mike Derer, 18; AP Photo/Morry Gash, 8; AP Photo/The Indianapolis Star, Kelly Wilkinson, 5; © D. Hurst/Alamy, 22; © Eric Lawton/Shutterstock, 41; © Haak78/Shutterstock, 6; © Jeff Morgan Alternative Technology/Alamy, 32; © Jim West/Alamy, 20, 21, 31; © Julien/Shutterstock, 17; © MWaits/Shutterstock, 15; © Photo Researchers, 11; © Plampy/Shutterstock, 37; © Rob Bouwman/Shutterstock, 36; © Vadim Koxlovsky/Alamy, 23; © Zack Frank/Alamy, 26

About the Author

Toney Allman holds degrees from Ohio State University and the University of Hawaii. She currently lives in Virginia, where she enjoys gardening, walks in the woods, and writing nonfiction books for students.